Oddities

poems by

Barbara Tramonte

Finishing Line Press
Georgetown, Kentucky

Oddities

Copyright © 2018 by Barbara Tramonte
ISBN 978-1-63534-368-7 First Edition
All rights reserved under International and Pan-American Copyright Conventions.
No part of this book may be reproduced in any manner whatsoever without written permission from the publisher, except in the case of brief quotations embodied in critical articles and reviews.

ACKNOWLEDGMENTS

Some of these poems have appeared or will appear in the following publications, to whose editors grateful acknowledgment is made:

Binnacle - "The Temporal Problem"
Boston Review - "Oddities"
Confluence - "It is 2:45 AM, AM"
Cutthroat - "To Le-Ann Who Had a Heart Attack"
Diverse Voices Quarterly - "The Ten Thousand Sorrow Living Room"
Eclipse: "A Woman's Past"
Eleven, Eleven - "A Chip Off the Old Block"
Frigg - Let Me Write About a Lady", "Here I Have"
Hiram Poetry Review - "La Vida"
Refugium, Poems for the Pacific - "Paint the Big Island"
Slipstream - "Green Is"
This Wood Sang Out - "The Sentence"
Tower Journal - "To Say"
Voices for Diversity and Social Justice, Rowman and Littlefield - "Language, The Truest Tongue"
Westview - "Travel"

Publisher: Leah Maines

Editor: Christen Kincaid

Cover Art: Deborah Harris

Author Photo: Ken Rosenfeld

Cover Design: Paris Miller

Printed in the USA on acid-free paper.
Order online: www.finishinglinepress.com
        also available on amazon.com

Author inquiries and mail orders:
Finishing Line Press
P. O. Box 1626
Georgetown, Kentucky 40324
U. S. A.

Table of Contents

1. Let me write about a lady
2. Language, the truest tongue
3. Travel
5. To Le-Ann who had a heart attack
6. Like a bolt
8. I sit in the bathroom
9. La Vida
10. A Woman's Past
11. Oddities
12. The Sentence
13. The ten thousand sorrow living room
14. Green Is
15. I have a lover
16. Dream on
17. The temporal problem
18. A Chip off the Old Block
19. The Day
20. To Say
22. What I feel
23. Imbabura
25. Why not?
26. Peggy
28. Warm Sheets
29. Do I like you?
30. Here I have
31. Paint the Big Island
34. It is 2:45 a.m.

For Rachel; poet and darling daughter

Let me write about a lady

In Mexico
Who lived on weed
And mushrooms
Mother creased and
Mother rises.

Let me tell of her time
In Oaxaca
Heating ebony pots
Near sunset
With mescal
In her feces.

I went into the museum there
And where the families stopped
With swaddling clothes,
He came!

Columbus,
With his short and pointed beard
His armor
And his metal way.

Let me tell
About the cistern
The mole
The nun's house
The way the Spanish carved
The town
Just like a carcass.

LANGUAGE, THE TRUEST TONGUE

A friend who teaches English in
New York City
is appalled!

One of her students writes,
"It's a doggy-dog world"
Another laments the fate of those
"who can't find they hats."

I bow to their genius,
they create their expression,
reveal their feelings with a metaphor
they own
not a borrowed one.

I've sat with Harvard grads and
felt like puking.
I've seen the way white people
brush the fate of Blacks off the table
like too many crumbs.

Hell, I've looked for work in New York City
down and out
and you know what Ms. B?
It's a doggy-dog world.

Travel

I am not Paul Bowles
Or a lady on a camel
Who loves the hump.
I travel in the Bronx
Dear dollar store
Hello, to Jelia Domingo
In Co-op City
Mon ami.

I travel to Brighton Beach
Hello, dear Russian lady with your
Lips and vodka beauty
I travel down your schmatta street
Beneath the el as
I am craning to be better.

Don't forget
Don't be afraid
I won't take you on a bleary
Borough bacchanalia
But we might stop at
Louis Armstrong's house
In Corona
To see his love for
Swiss Kriss
And all life.

I travel to a stoop on 64th
Where a beggar asks for money
And I give it.
He gives it back
And asks if I can
Buy a meal for him
At "Eat Here Now".

He says that Bernie Madoff
Sometimes gave him change for food.
He points to Bernie's pad above, then grins
"I didn't know he was a thief."

To Le-Ann who had a heart attack

On New Year's Eve
My student
Legally blind

Had a heart attack
But that was after her eviction
Now she's in rehab
Submitting her Master's Thesis
To me for
Our 16th iteration

To Le-Ann, who had a heart attack
On New Year's Eve
Who has more fight in her
Than a drill to the earth

Who I carry like a wounded sack
Of mashed up innards
Who will finish
Or finish me

To Le-Ann, berating me
Commanding that I read
Re-read, re-tread, explain
Why I can't make the world right
Why she is blind
Why her daughter's on the spectrum
Why her veteran status
Can't save her from the streets
Why Schlossberg's theory of transition
Means shit in real life.

Like a bolt

I am here
Electrified
OK, lit up

But I come as
A griot
To tell you a tale
Of recollection

On a hot summer street
Brooklyn street
Heat from concrete rose
From underneath

I was a tadpole
A frog, a snake
A fly- trap for cotton candy
A caramel
With the widest mouth
That was me

Ramona and Pippi
And Nancy Drew

I was dancing down the street
I had a bandanna
A fake horse and
The wind beneath me

You let me wander those streets so young
Those streets made me, built me
You let me know the world
The bakery, the kittens
The scary neighbors
The smelly ones
The synagogue
The street games
The cherry pits
The chairs
That folded.

I sit in the bathroom

I sit in the bathroom writing
It is steamy. David bathes
  with boats and soldiers.
He's freezing. "Make it hotter Ma."

He is a beauty beyond the spell of marble
penis, thighs, stretch of blonde shag
mouth wide as a river.
He is on course.

I can only nod, Yes, Yes, Yes.

"Can I have toys?"
Yes.

"Can I eat candy?"
Yes.

Can I watch violent TV shows?
Yes. Yes. Yes.
        You decide.

La Vida

Living with midriff bulge?
Eating hamburgers
and sodden pizza crusts?
Lying on paper lined
leatherettes
at the doctor's office?

How many people
stick their finger up *your* vagina?

Make deadlines
rush home
tend babies, parents, sisters.
Live on record, for what?

All digits on keys
pecking like dirty pigeons to
tell the story of Aunt Ida,
my cousin Mimi, my first reptilian pet
from the Berkshires.
(She shriveled in a bucket.)

I may never stop these stories
like Persian rugs
repeating patterns
spread by a sweeping
lizard's tongue
trying to locate
how the wind blows
or when to varnish
the loom.

A Woman's Past

There was the unconscious play-acting
Of a young girl
Stripped bare of motives.
There was the youthful stride from
Toothpick
To swirling shapes men dream of.
She carried it.
At first like a package to be delivered.
Then, like goods she owned.
These possessions
Began to tap directions
With the nerve of a blind man's cane.
Take me here
Get me this
Forget what you were thinking
And find what you are groping for.

The woman glances back
And sees the girl unconscious.
Could sex be tied to consciousness,
the first real perception we make?
The girl playing stoop ball
With hair a barrette won't hold
Doesn't really know why the eyes of men
Define her,
But her meaning changes in the arc
Of what they see.

Oddities

A dog runs after everything you throw
Not so, a tiger
A tiger runs for the throat
Of the person
Throwing

Good tiger
Smart tiger
I adore you

I run at you
Savage
Masticating
Carnal

If I rip you open
I will die

THE SENTENCE

The sentence is in the forgetting
and in the rude pin prick of awakening
at electronic intervals, for maximum
pain best achieved when we are dozing off.

I love you at the beach,
In Chinatown
at a whole hog barbecue.
Drinking strong coffee,
reading Wordsworth
declaring, no screaming, your
happiness.

I love you when you cant,
chant, bore and regale me with
the history of circumcision
and swing hard to manhood.

Even though we've forgotten,
the sentence comes our way.
Passed to us on a torn slip of paper.
Hey, cool lovers, it's your turn now.

The ten thousand sorrow living room

I swab
the hurt of missing you
with chenille and shabby chic
The rooms will save me
The pots and woven rugs
Artifacts made with care
by human hands that
turned sorrow into objects
of cloth
and clay and
bulging orbs
of consolation.

Green Is

Green is the new gray
Boys are the new flotation devices
Girls remain the same

Sixty is the new thirty
Sex, the new kiss

Steeples are the new staples
Food, the new enemy
Guns remain the same

Sixty is the new thirty

More fathers fuck daughters
Or fuck them over
Microfiber means no ironing
Sex is the new handshake
Girls and guns and bad relationships
Are the new farms?
And cheating means you win.

I HAVE A LOVER

I have a lover, another
another, another
He is huggy, bristly
Short yet lanky
He is so intellectual
My mind wrings itself
He is not, but he is
Beautiful and smart in ways that
Don't fit books
He breaks the binding
He is smart but not
Philosophical
Most things are clear
He is like a model airplane
Pilot with a shearling cap
Who said such sunken cheeks
Should be ignored?
He is pretty shy, but takes
Me to Jamaica
He is waiting but I'll
Never get there
I see that I am finite
I won't make it.

Dream on

With me, heart
Two A.M.
Dream in ways
The phone book
Never knew

There was snow
A fresh fall
Of quiet Nagasaki
In that moment
When the blanket
Fixed everything

We must obey the law
Of latent ideas
When they grow like pumpkins
These laws have members and
In the first place
We knew it would go this way

Secondly, they unfold
With 3-D clichés
Did we really believe
There were only
Three dimensions?

True ancestor of my tribal body
Times two
Because each person cannot stand alone

The temporal problem

How to go on
While monks with bells
Chant monkey mind?

How to absorb and then
Propel the thought
Of your mother dying
To calm acceptance
At an Italian restaurant
You frequented with her
While she lived

How to understand the ghosts
Of each experience
Playing ski-ball with abandon
Hanging on a stoop
Tongue kissing
Joe McQueen

Walking home, getting
Picked up by a guy who looked like Bud
From Father Knows Best
But drove a gas delivery truck

Entering your parent's house
Small, modest,
Beverley Road
Lying bold- faced
To your skulking dad
That Bonnie walked you home.

A Chip off the Old Block

Every time I go to my dentist
He looks at my dwindling teeth
And shouts, "She has teeth just like her father!"

Yes! He knew my father
But did he know
The blood and iron of his ways?

Yes! He knew my father
His teeth
His checkbook
His less than desirable
Gag reflex
But did he know
The way he ground me down
Until I whimpered?
Recollecting that is filled with shame.

So, every time I go to my dentist
Which is quite often with my cracks and
Fissures, root canals and losses
I want to respond to his progenitor observation
Yes! I have teeth like my father
But you should see my dick.

The Day

Arise
Happy, so happy
Chirp serotonin
On a train

Time goes by
But I am not whistling
I am in a culvert
Whose sides scrape my skin

Sleep comes
She says, hello there, boys

Wake up
Must edit poems
Collate poems
Digitize poems
Rake them
Snake and stake them

I am a small figure
Purring over my poems

Wondering how this day could be
So long.

To Say

We are your son and
daughters
Yours, truly yours.
Could there ever be
A cadre of children
More devoted?
Could there ever be a son
And daughters
Wrapped in shawls or
Jacketed strictly in twill
Dedicated
To the teardrops of your
Wind and fire?

We come to your bed mother
Like lemmings to a bog
Like Brooklynites coming home
From work
From imaginary fields and
Real factories and
Gum popping estuaries near
Street corners, aunts
And Idas and Smokey Joes

We come to your bed
Like children with pea pods
In our chests
With Coney Island in our hearts
With remembrances of diapers
And diaphragms pinned like
Butterfly constructions.

We come mother
Like zombies from the last hundred years
Like lake lizards recently hatched
Like hungry mouths
And scraped corner toes
Like all we knew once before
To say mother
To say Brooklyn
To say we come
We come
To say mother.

What I feel

As I soothe
My mother
Here, old lady
Indian
Princess
Devi
Shakti
Carnation
Of birth possibilities
Now hunch
And scrabble
With thin bones
Thin body
Here, old mother
Serpent turtle
Mahalo
Catchment, otter
Wallet
Wool that kissed a needle
With desire
Here, Grande Dame with
Feathered hat
And hair pinned in an aerial way.
As silly as
The fence
The rose upon the fence
The edge of land held tightly by the fence
The never-ending boundary of
The fence.

Imbabura

El presidente
Weaves with his body
Like a spider
Women wash clothing
In a river of tears
Animals defecate
And look confused
At the market

"It took me seven days
to weave this rug."
Whole families knit
And laugh
People
Blow breath
Into reeds and pipes
Sing songs
The mountain taught

Wrapped in blankets
With babies on their backs
People caught
Between Latin
And the earth

Girls wear white blouses
With flowers reiterating
Their grandmothers' stories
On a yoke of real dreams

There is a bridge that Indians make
That cannot be walked
There is an arc
Beyond the passport

Of the west
That spans the mountains
Sips river cocktails in the afternoon

Something Chinese
Or aphrodisiac
Lemon verbena

Tomato tree
Naranjilla
Hair that spins cables for bridges

When you smile, Ecuador
You sit in my lap

Llamas, dogs that drool,
Horse blankets
Women with hair like
Puzzles that mock and
Unlock police uniforms
In the street.

Why not?

Lean on me
And allow
My attendant
Sickness so you can
See how to grow old

Look at me head on
With your eyes like Google eyes
And your masts in the virtual wind

I cannot stop you
I don't know how
Any more
Than I can
Refute that the longer
We live
The more pain

Here is my case
Judge and jury
For cutting it short
This life

I wanted
Nothing flimsy
Nothing gone too fast
Only us, with our fractious bulge and
Cryptic signage
Our span
Spun in lace in
This life
Right now

Peggy

I know you through Maureen
Of the dimples
And determined step

I know you through the evenings
Drinking wine
Extolling potatoes
Expressing onion love

Peggy
You are a beautiful
Spiritual orb
In a sea of commerce

A lady among beasts

Having dinner with you tonight
On your near-death made my heart sing
For the strength
Of your dear spindly self

You went, at six years old
With a clutched fist of money
On the bus from Everett to Boston
To pay your father's bills

Back then, in the 1920s,
People thought children
Were people

Fathers let kids know the struggle

Dinner with Peggy:
The crux of
A prayer
To say
In private

For all of us
May we go
With her fire and grace

Warm Sheets

I am in Florida in warm sheets
They are clean
And my son is near me
There are people of my blood
Who hold me
And we know each other
As screws know hinges
Suction cups; cold glass.
There is my son
Handsome warlord who has needed
Me beyond his own strength
There is my daughter
A spirit of puns and wry insights
She knows the setting
On Anne Sexton's dial.
There are sisters and lovers
A mother
A man who wed me with
Courageous assurance
After the subway roared
After the needle braised my arm
After the confusion of bricks and windows
Led to no fire escape.

Do I like you?

When I am with you
I do not feel at ease
Yet, over and over
I engage and
Make appointments
So I can come through
A beaver searching wood
A gerbil looks for cardboard
A tool
For taking sweater pills away
I will be there
Drinking
Eating quenelles
Or wasabi and
Dreaming crystal meth

But guess what?
I don't really like you
And I never felt at ease
Around your skeevy presence

But I still need to connect with you
To teeter on a barstool next to you
To play piano on a QWERTY keyboard
To sigh
With a type of Russian
Exasperation and desire.

Here I have

Hannah on this night
In New York City
Totally mine
Hannah

Here I have Hannah
Baba, I can read!
Miracle of miracles
Brain of mysterious
Brain. She can read.
Here she is, Hannah.
A waif, a girl in my girl's
Skin. A grand and very daughter.
Hannah.

Here she flaunts herself
In front of my upper east side
Mirror. Baba, look,
My hair has grown.

Paint the Big Island

With words

Tell about the walk
To the tide pool
In a way
That screams cadmium
And *hala* tree flowers
On the path
Past the lookout
To the sea

Tell of your arduous walk
In Japanese fisherman shoes
With felt bottoms
Down a cinder path
Where after the railing ends
You are on your own
Against a terrifying landscape

Come out of the forest
With its snarling undergrowth
Geckos as green as chartreuse

Face the sea

You can't get down to the sea
Until you climb the lava rocks
Some steep, some jagged
A payment for your soles

You grapple;
Up, down
Frantic for footing
While a young bare chested
Man holding a baby in one hand

And a beer bottle in the other
(With a cigarette in his mouth}
Traverses the rocks like they've been
Laid smooth by the
Department of Public Works

You go on all fours
In your skirted bathing suit
While your lovely old sisters
Strike a pose in their hats

Look up

Even if this threatens your footing
You scream inside
At the sight of the tide pool
Waves swell, smash
Coming, coming, coming
A crystalline blue
A Tiffany blue
Before they break
And flood the pool

Find your spot

Grip smooth rocks
Slick with sea moss
They talk to you
As the salt
Seeps into your body

The sun is on your hair

Between you and
The vast Pacific
Just rocks

You are small
You are in a skirted bathing suit
Maybe years go by
Before this impossible sea
Before these volcanic rocks
Before you ever knew anything
It all slips away.

It is 2:45 a.m.

It is 2:45 a.m.
a.m., a.m.
Ordinarily we'd have
tea now.
We would dig up portions
of our souls from the night
and plant them in each other.
Twisting squash flowers
with heavy stems
low to the ground,
fields of cosmos, patches of lavender,
fragrant oregano, mint -
All this we'd become.
Now I am up at 2:45 a.m.
a.m., a.m.
and there is no ordinary thing to do.
There is the deepness of silence,
the earth with no root,
the cup with no lip.

www.ingramcontent.com/pod-product-compliance
Lightning Source LLC
LaVergne TN
LVHW041556070426
835507LV00011B/1118